SHORT WALKS
BANNAU BRYCHEINIOG

BRECON BEACONS

by Andy Davies

Patchwork of improved fields in the Usk Valley (Walks 9–11)

CONTENTS

Using this guide.. 4
Route summary table 6
Map key 7
Introduction... 9
   Walking in Bannau Brycheiniog..................................... 10
   Things to see and do 10
   Where to stay... 11
   Travel 11

The walks
1.	Henrhyd Falls	13
2.	Waterfall Country: Elidir Trail	17
3.	Waterfall Country: Four Waterfalls Walk	23
4.	Craig Cerrig-gleisiad	29
5.	Pen y Fan	35
6.	Llyn Cwm Llwch	39
7.	Cwm Sere	45
8.	Blaen-y-glyn waterfalls	51
9.	Pencelli canal walk	55
10.	Canal, Usk Valley and Afon Caerfanell	61
11.	River Usk, canal and Llangynidr Bridge	67
12.	Craig y Cilau	71
13.	Table Mountain	79
14.	Sugar Loaf	83
15.	Ysgyryd Fawr (Skirrid Mountain)	89

Useful information... 94

USING THIS GUIDE

Routes in this book

In this book you will find a selection of easy or moderate walks suitable for almost everyone, including casual walkers and families with children, or for when you only have a short time to fill. The routes have been carefully chosen to allow you to explore the area and its attractions. Most routes are circular or out-and-back, although some linear walks may be included that use public transport to get back to the start. Although there may be some climbs there is no challenging terrain, but do bear in mind that conditions can sometimes be wet or muddy underfoot. A route summary table is included on page 6 to help you choose the right walk.

Clothing and footwear

You won't need any special equipment to enjoy these walks. The weather in Britain can be changeable, so choose clothing suitable for the season and wear or carry a waterproof jacket. For footwear, comfortable walking boots or trainers with a good grip are best. A small rucksack for drinks, snacks and spare clothing is useful. See www.adventuresmart.uk.

Walk descriptions

At the beginning of each walk you'll find all the information you need:

- start/finish location, with a what3words address to help you find it
- parking and transport information, estimated walking time, total distance and climb
- details of public toilets available along the route and where you can get refreshments
- a summary of the key highlights of the walk and what you might see

Timings given are the time to complete the walk at a reasonable walking pace. Allow extra time for extended stops or if walking with children.

The route is described in clear, easy-to-follow directions, with each waypoint marked on an accompanying map extract. It's a good idea to read the whole of the route instructions before setting out, so that you know what to expect.

Maps, GPX files and what3words

Extracts from the OS® 1:25,000 map accompany each route. GPX files for all the walks in this book are available to download at www.cicerone.co.uk/1235/gpx.

What3words is a free smartphone app which identifies every 3m square of the globe with a unique three-word address, e.g. ///destiny.cafe.sonic. For more information see https://what3words.com/products/what3words-app.

USING THIS GUIDE

Walking with children

Even young children can be surprisingly strong walkers, but every family is different and you may need to adapt the timings given in this book to take that into account. Make sure you go at the pace of the slowest member and choose a walk with an exciting objective in mind, such as a cave, river, waterfall or picnic spot. Many of the walks can be shortened to suit – suggestions are included at the end of the route description.

Dogs

Sheep or cattle may be found grazing on a number of these walks. Keep dogs under control at all times so that they don't scare or disturb livestock or wildlife. Cattle, particularly cows with calves, may very occasionally pose a risk to walkers with dogs. If you ever feel threatened by cattle, you should let go of your dog's lead and let it run free.

Enjoying the countryside responsibly

Enjoy the countryside and treat it with respect to protect our natural environments. Stick to footpaths and take your litter home with you. When driving, slow down on rural roads and park considerately, or better still use public transport. For more details check out www.gov.uk/countryside-code.

The Countryside Code

Respect everyone
- be considerate to those living in, working in and enjoying the countryside
- leave gates and property as you find them
- do not block access to gateways or driveways when parking
- be nice, say hello, share the space
- follow local signs and keep to marked paths unless wider access is available

Protect the environment
- take your litter home – leave no trace of your visit
- do not light fires and only have BBQs where signs say you can
- always keep dogs under control and in sight
- dog poo – bag it and bin it – any public waste bin will do
- care for nature – do not cause damage or disturbance

Enjoy the outdoors
- check your route and local conditions
- plan your adventure – know what to expect and what you can do
- enjoy your visit, have fun, make a memory

ROUTE SUMMARY TABLE

WALK NAME	START POINT	TIME	DISTANCE
1. Henrhyd Falls	Layby on A4067, Ynyswen	1¾hr	5.5km (3½ miles)
2. Waterfall Country: Elidir Trail	Pontneddfechan	2hr	6km (3¾ miles)
3. Waterfall Country: Four Waterfalls Walk	Cwm Porth car park	2hr	8km (5 miles)
4. Craig Cerrig-gleisiad	Layby on A470	2hr	5.5km (3½ miles)
5. Pen y Fan	Pont ar Daf car park	3½hr	7.5km (4¾ miles)
6. Llyn Cwm Llwch	Nant Cwm Llwch car park	2hr	8km (5 miles)
7. Cwm Sere	Cwm Gwdi car park	2hr	5.5km (3½ miles)
8. Blaen-y-glyn waterfalls	Blaen-y-glyn Isaf car park	1½hr	4km (2½ miles)
9. Pencelli canal walk	Pencelli	2½hr	9km (5½ miles)
10. Canal, Usk Valley and Afon Caerfanell	Talybont-on-Usk	2½hr	9km (5½ miles)
11. River Usk, canal and Llangynidr Bridge	Llangynidr	2¼hr	7.5km (4¾ miles)
12. Craig y Cilau	Llangattock Quarry car park	2hr	7km (4¼ miles)
13. Table Mountain	Crickhowell	2hr	6km (3¾ miles)
14. Sugar Loaf	Road end north of Abergavenny	3hr	8km (5 miles)
15. Ysgyryd Fawr (Skirrid Mountain)	The Skirrid car park	2hr	5km (3 miles)

ROUTE SUMMARY TABLE

HIGHLIGHTS
Waterfall, river and gorge
Waterfalls, river and gorge
Cave, waterfalls, river and gorge
Glacial cwm, wildlife
Highest summit in South Wales, views
Mythical lake, waterfalls, glacial valley
Spectacular glacial valley, Iron Age settlement
Hanging valley, waterfalls and river
Canal and wildlife
River, canal and industrial heritage
River, canal and wildlife
Nature reserve, caves, industrial heritage
Iron Age hill fort and panorama
Woodland, summit and panorama
Summit and panorama

SYMBOLS USED ON ROUTE MAPS

- **S** — Start point
- **F** — Finish point
- **SF** — Start and finish at the same place
- **4 ▶** — Waypoint
- 〜 — Route line

MAPPING IS SHOWN AT A SCALE OF 1:25,000

0 KM — 0.25 — 0.5
0 miles — 0.25

DOWNLOAD THE GPX FILES FOR FREE AT

www.cicerone.co.uk/1235/gpx

Walking through the woodland at Graig Llech to Henrhyd Falls (Walk 1)

INTRODUCTION

Sgwd yr Eira on the Afon Hepste in the Waterfall Country (Walk 3)

Situated in an unspoilt area of South Wales, just north of the former coal-mining valleys, Bannau Brycheiniog National Park is a place of beautiful and diverse landscapes. It was formerly known as the Brecon Beacons but was renamed in 2023, with Bannau meaning 'peaks' and Brycheiniog referring to King Brychan who ruled over a 5th-century kingdom that encompassed the area. One of three national parks in Wales, more than half of its 1344km² lie at over 305m above sea level, and it is blessed with a rich mixture of majestic valleys, dramatic waterfalls, and high mountain peaks and ridges.

The Bannau Brycheiniog National Park falls naturally into four geographic areas. These are (from west to east): Mynydd Du (the Black Mountain), Fforest Fawr (the Great Forest), the Bannau Brycheiniog (Brecon Beacons) and the Black Mountains (Y Mynyddoedd Duon). These all have different characters, making this area unique in offering such varied walking experiences.

The rocks that form most of the national park are red in colour and formed when this area was part of a giant supercontinent called Pangea. Light grey Carboniferous limestone rocks are found in the southern part of the national park. These dissolve slowly in acidic rainwater giving rise to spectacular caves where rivers can disappear underground for many

River Usk at the bridge in Crickhowell

kilometres. Millions of years ago tectonic forces squashed and bent the rocks into mountains and they were then sculpted by the last Ice Age, creating the U-shaped valleys and glacial lakes we see today.

Walking in Bannau Brycheiniog

The walks in this guide cater for most abilities and interests, and cover the areas of Fforest Fawr, the Bannau Brycheiniog (Brecon Beacons) and the Black Mountains (Y Mynyddoedd Duon). Each walk has a special feature to discover, including waterfalls, woodland, tranquil U-shaped valleys, canals, rivers and panoramic viewpoints. The routes are all circular or out-and-back walks, and generally make use of well-marked paths. The mountain routes can involve some steep sections, while the challenge route (Walk 5) ascends Pen y Fan, the highest peak in South Wales at 886m. The walks in the Waterfall Country (Walks 2 and 3) can be muddy and slippery in places, and the numerous cascades can change from clear water tumbling serenely over rocky bands in fine weather to raging torrents after heavy rain. There are a few steep drops so take care if you are walking with children.

Things to see and do

There are plenty of things to see and activities for visitors of all ages and tastes, making the national park a great place for families to visit. Favourite attractions for children include the Dan-yr-Ogof Show Caves in the Swansea Valley, the Brecon Mountain Railway at Penderyn and the Big Pit National Coal Museum near Blaenavon.

Several picturesque market towns lie on the edges of the park, such as Llandovery, Brecon, Crickhowell and Abergavenny, and these are also great places to explore. Both the River Usk and the tree-lined Brecon and Monmouthshire Canal that runs alongside the it provides opportunities for a leisurely walk of variable length, and there are numerous unspoilt old pubs to enjoy – the Skirrid Mountain Inn is reputed to be one of the oldest in Wales. There is also a tavern in the undercroft of Llanthony Priory.

Where to stay

The towns of Brecon, Crickhowell and Abergavenny lie along the Usk Valley and are excellent bases from which to explore the park. There is a wide variety of accommodation along the corridor formed by the Usk Valley, from hotels on country estates to self-catering cottages on the mountain slopes. Brecon is the main hub and has supermarkets, while the smaller centres of Crickhowell and Abergavenny have shops with excellent local produce.

Travel

The Bannau Brycheiniog National Park is a day trip from Swansea, Cardiff, Bristol and the Midlands and an ideal short-break destination from London, only 200km (120 miles) away. The park is linked to the rail network at Abergavenny by the Welsh Marches Line that runs from Newport to Hereford and on to the Midlands, and Merthyr Tydfil is linked to Cardiff which has frequent trains from London.

There are excellent motorway links with the rest of the UK, with the A40 in the east linking with the M50, and the A4042 from Newport, A470 from Cardiff and A465 from Neath and Swansea all connected by the M4.

The river and canal walks in the Usk Valley (Walks 9–11) are accessible by bus from Brecon, Crickhowell and Abergavenny. A bus also serves the Pen y Fan walk (Walk 5) linking Brecon to Merthyr Tydfil along the A470. The Henrhyd Falls walk (Walk 1) is on a bus route along the Swansea Valley. A car is essential for accessing the other walks, and the ones that enter the northern valleys involve driving along narrow, if quiet, country lanes. The car park for the walk to the summit of Pen y Fan fills up quickly, as does the available parking in Cwm Porth in the Waterfall Country.

Family starting their walk in Cwm Llwch (Walk 6)

Henrhyd Falls

WALK 1
Henrhyd Falls

Start/finish	Layby on A4067 at Ynyswen
Locate	///custard.steadier.laminate
Cafes/pubs	Pubs in Abercrave (550m off route)
Transport	Bus service from Brecon to Swansea stops 170m east of layby
Parking	Layby on A4067 at Ynyswen (SA9 1FG), or in village of Abercrave
Toilets	No public toilets on route

Time 1¾hr
Distance 5.5km (3½ miles)
Climb 110m

Ascend the intimate gorge of Nant Llech to reach the highest waterfall in South Wales

This is an out-and-back route that ascends gently through a wooded gorge carved out by Nant Llech to Henrhyd Falls, the highest cascade in South Wales at 27m. The path follows alongside the stream at first and then climbs high up on the wooded valley side. The falls were used as the entrance to the Batcave in the 2012 film *The Dark Knight Rises*. It is possible to walk behind the curtain of water but take care as the wet rocks are slippery.

View from behind Henrhyd Falls

River Tawe at the footbridge

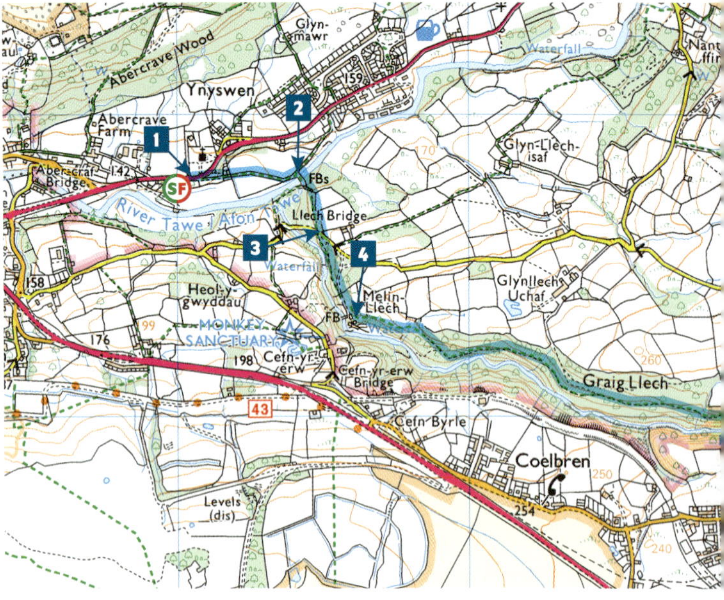

WALK 1 – HENRHYD FALLS

1 From the layby on the bend on the A4067 walk a short distance along the road to a point opposite the graveyard at **St David's Church**. Turn right and follow the waymarked track that descends to a house. A path continues to the right to the **River Tawe** and a bridge.

2 Cross this and ascend the steps up to the left, ignoring the wooden bridge across Nant Llech on the right. Go through the kissing gate and follow the path through the woodland along the bank of the stream at first and then climb to the road.

3 Turn right and then leave the road to the left on the path that leads along the gorge of Nant Llech. You soon reach the riverbank where you have a good view of the rock strata that tilt or dip upstream, creating small waterfalls. You can appreciate why Nant Llech means 'rock slab stream'.

Look out for damp-loving vegetation growing on the rocks, boulders and tree branches, as Nant Llech is a Site of Special Scientific Interest for its wide range of rare mosses, ferns, lichens and liverworts.

ⓘ *The name of the national park was changed in 2023 from the 'Brecon Beacons' to 'Bannau Brycheiniog'. Bannau means peaks and Brycheiniog refers to the name of a medieval kingdom that covered the area.*

Waterfall on the Nant Llech near Melin Llech

The path meets a track coming down from the left. Turn right, continuing along the gorge to a wooden bridge.

> ⓘ **Sgwd** *is Welsh for waterfall and means to toss or fling.*

4 Do not cross but continue along the left-hand side of the valley to a ruined stone building, **Melin Llech**, which was once a woollen mill. Continue along the path passing a National Trust sign for Sgwd Henrhyd to where a track joins from the left.

5 Bear right here and continue through **Graig Llech** to a wooden bridge across the main river. In the winter you get a glimpse of the fall further up the gorge. Cross over and ascend the wooden steps on the other side to reach **Henrhyd Falls** on the south bank. It is possible to walk behind the fall but take care as the rocks are slippery.

6 Retrace your steps back to the start.

Sgwd Henrhyd

Sgwd Henrhyd (Henrhyd Falls) has a vertical drop of 27m, making it the highest waterfall in South Wales. Earth movements along a geological fault 300 million years ago brought the hard sandstone of the Farewell Rock adjacent to the softer, easily eroded Coal Measure shales that normally lie above. The water has worn away the soft shales at a faster rate than the sandstone, resulting in a step in the riverbed. Over thousands of years, the size of the step increased as the shale at the base of the waterfall was worn away, and the overhanging Farewell Rock collapsed to produce a spectacular gorge and high waterfall.

Henrhyd Falls lit by the evening sun

WALK 2
Waterfall Country: Elidir Trail

Time 2hr
Distance 6km (3¾ miles)
Climb 75m

An easy route to wonderful waterfalls, past industry and a fairy kingdom

Start/finish	Bridge in Pontneddfechan
Locate	///puncture.prowess.caskets
Cafes/pubs	Pubs in Pontneddfechan
Transport	Pontneddfechan is on the Neath to Merthyr Tydfil bus route
Parking	On street in the village but fills up quickly on busy days
Toilets	In Pontneddfechan

The Elidir Trail takes in the beautiful riverside scenery of the Afon Pyrddin and Afon Nedd. It includes several impressive waterfalls which are usually at their best when the rivers are in full spate. The river geology is interesting and there is also evidence of old industrial and mining activity in the valley along the route. You may even come across the entrance to the fairy kingdom!

Sgwd Ddwil Isaf on the Nedd Fechan

SHORT WALKS BANNAU BRYCHEINIOG

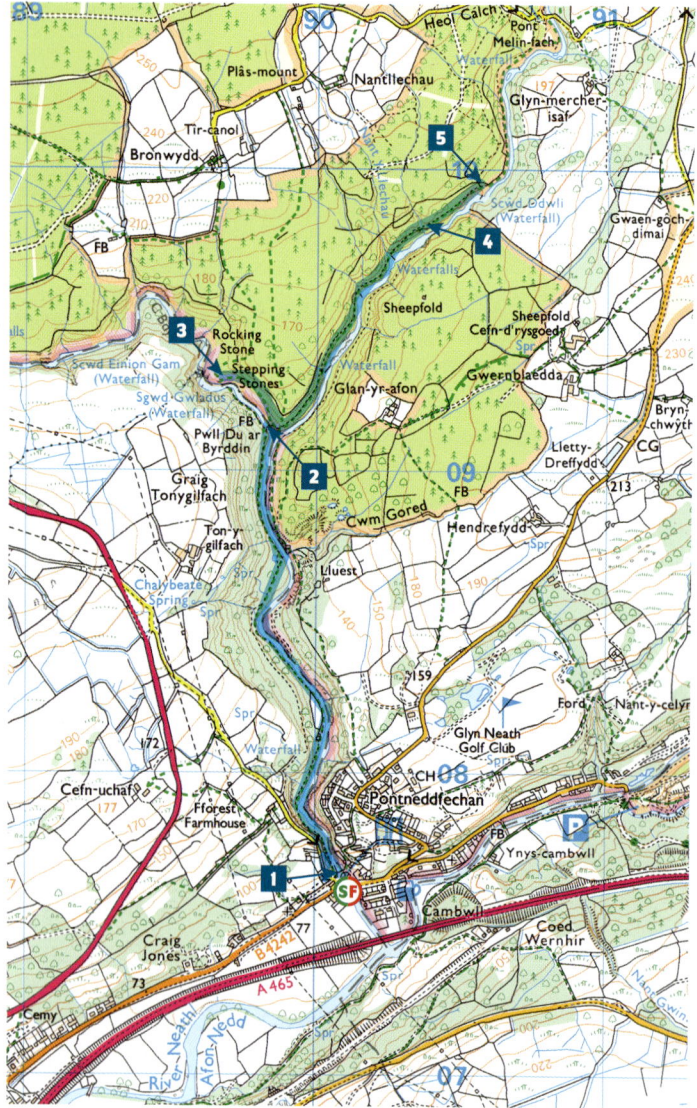

WALK 2 – WATERFALL COUNTRY: ELIDIR TRAIL

1 Start at the bridge across the **Afon Nedd** where a wrought-iron sign indicates that the path leads to the White Lady Falls (Sgwd Gwladus). Follow the wide track – once a tramway for transporting silica – for just over 1.5km up the side of the river to a bridge. The mine adits along the track were once used to extract silica for making fire bricks. The rock was also used for making millstones.

Sgwd y Bedol on the Nedd Fechan

2 Cross the bridge and turn left, following the right bank of the Afon Pyrddin to **Sgwd Gwladus** waterfall.

> Gwladys was the daughter of the 5th-century king Brychan of Brycheiniog, who had 24 daughters and 12 sons! Brychan was, unusually for his time, of Gaelic or Irish descent.

3 Retrace your steps back to the bridge but do not cross and instead bear left up the gorge formed by the Afon Nedd to Sgwd y Bedol (Horseshoe Fall), a further 1km from the bridge. Continue ahead to approach **Scwd Ddwli Isaf** either via the flat rocks in the riverbed (if the water is low) or by a track up to the left if they are covered. The falls are in two sections, the second part being higher than the first and in an area enclosed by cliffs.

4 To continue upstream, retrace your steps along the stream bed for about 20m to the end of the crags and scramble up the slope to gain the path above and continue along the path to **Scwd Ddwli Uchaf** waterfall. Ddwli means 'gushing' and these falls really live up to their name when in spate.

5 Turn around here and retrace your steps back to the bridge. Cross over and back along the track to the start.

> **– To shorten**
>
> Just visit Sgwd Gwladus and retrace your route back to the start without going along the Nedd Fechan. This saves 3.5km (1hr).

Sgwd Gwladus on the Afon Pyrddin when the fall froze in 2009

WALK 2 – WATERFALL COUNTRY: ELIDIR TRAIL

Sgwd Ddwli Uchaf on the Nedd Fechan

From the Travels of Giraldus Cambrensis

Giraldus Cambrensis, son of a Norman Baron and a Welsh Princess, wrote Itinerarium Cambriae (The Journey through Wales) in the late 12th century. One of the stories he recorded was about Elidyr, after which this trail is named. In the 4th century, Elidyr, aged 12, was beaten by his teacher, so he ran away and hid under the banks of the Afon Nedd. As he crouched there, hungry and miserable, two tiny men appeared and took him through a tunnel to a land where all was playtime and pleasure. Elidyr became friends with the king's son but frequently returned to the upper world where he told only his mother of his adventures.

His mother asked him to bring her back a present of gold, a common metal in the land. Elidyr returned with a golden ball, which he stole while playing with the king's son. When he tripped on the doorstep of his house, the little people caught up with him, snatching the ball and running off with it, scorning Elidyr. Realising his foolish act, Elidyr ran back to the river but the entrance to the tunnel had gone.

Sgwd yr Eira (The Fall of Snow) on the Afon Hepste

WALK 3
Waterfall Country: Four Waterfalls Walk

Start/finish	*Cwm Porth car park*
Locate	*///risen.noises.scrolled*
Cafes/pubs	*None on route*
Transport	*No public transport*
Parking	*Cwm Porth National Park pay-and-display car park (CF44 9JF)*
Toilets	*At car park*

Time 2hr
Distance 8km (5 miles)
Climb 185m

Walk behind a curtain of water as the Afon Hepste plunges into space over your head

This is the classic waterfall walk, taking in four major cascades in the Waterfall Country and culminating in an unforgettable experience of walking behind a sizeable waterfall. Autumn is the best season to visit, as the deciduous woods will be a riot of colour, and the warm summer months are an opportunity take a dip in one of the many inviting pools. There is one steep section on the descent to Sgwd yr Eira.

Resurgence pool on the Afon Mellte

SHORT WALKS BANNAU BRYCHEINIOG

1 Before setting off visit **Porth yr Ogof** cave entrance next to the car park in the river valley below. Porth yr Ogof is the largest cave entrance in Wales through which the Afon Mellte disappears underground into an extensive cave system. After you have visited the cave, go to the lower car park exit and straight across the road onto the footpath through the woodland.

At post marker 87 you can make a short detour down to the Blue Pool, where the Afon Mellte emerges from a cave entrance. Do not be tempted to go for a swim – the underwater currents are treacherous and several people have lost their lives here.

Continue through the woodland to a grassy open area and to the bank of the **Afon Mellte**. Turn left and follow the river downstream to a bridge.

2 Do not cross the bridge but follow the green waymarked path that climbs diagonally up the slope through woodland to meet the red waymarked path at fingerpost 12. Turn right (signed 'Sgwd yr Eira') and turn right again at fingerpost 13 to make the short two-minute excursion to a viewing area of **Sgwd Clun-gwyn**.

The waterfall was formed by earth movements bringing soft shales into contact with much tougher sandstone. The river wore away the weak shales but the harder

Entrance to Porth yr Ogof cave

WALK 3 – WATERFALL COUNTRY: FOUR WATERFALLS WALK

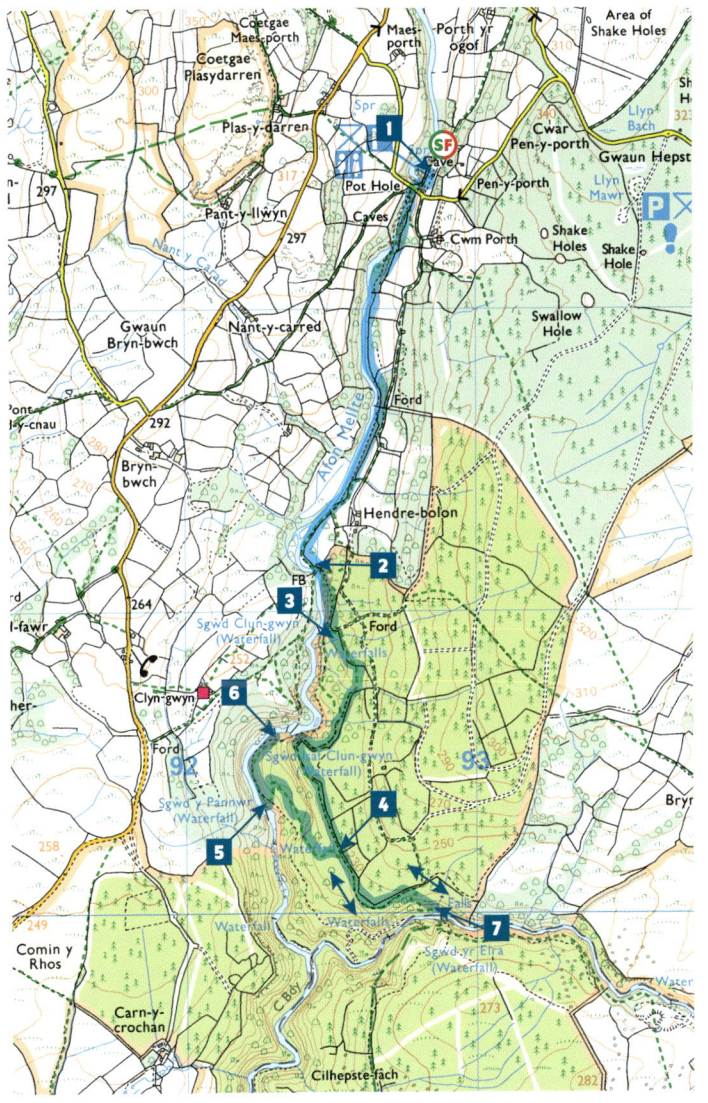

Ancient woodland along the Mellte gorge

sandstone resisted, leaving the impressive step over which the water plunges into space today.

3 Return to the main path and continue above the gorge for 1km to fingerpost 25.

4 Turn right on a green link path to the 12m high **Sgwd y Pannwr**. Meaning 'Fall of the Fuller', the fuller's job was to use the power of the falling water to wash sheep's wool and make it shrink to produce softer cloth.

5 Take the path upstream of the fall to the base of **Sgwd Isaf Clun-gwyn**. Sgwd Isaf Clun-gwyn was also formed by movement along fractures in the earth's crust with the soft shales being washed away and the harder rocks again forming the complex cascade.

6 Go back to **Swgd y Pannwr** and climb out of the gorge by retracing your steps and turn right when you rejoin the path. The route then swings east along the top of the Hepste gorge to fingerpost 35. Turn right here and descend the steps to **Sgwd yr Eira**. The Welsh name translates as The Fall of Snow.

WALK 3 – WATERFALL COUNTRY: FOUR WATERFALLS WALK

7 Retrace your steps back along the top of the gorge to the start after exploring behind the fall if the river is not in spate and it is safe to do so.

> **– To shorten**
> Just visit as many falls as you wish then return to the start.

Sgwd yr Eira

Of all the falls in the Bannau Brycheiniog National Park, this is the most exciting to visit. Notice when you stand behind the fall that your feet are on hard sandstone but that the rocks in a recessed band at the base of the cliff are relatively weak, thinly bedded shales that crumble away easily. The rocks above are of a more resistant sandstone but are weakened by numerous bedding planes. The final massive band of sandstone, which forms the protruding shelf over which the water tumbles, is the strongest and so is the most resistant to collapse, resulting in the fall being thrown out spectacularly into space.

Sgwd Isaf Clun-gwyn

View of Pen y Fan and Corn Du from the top of the cliffs

WALK 4
Craig Cerrig-gleisiad

Time 2hr
Distance 5.5km (3½ miles)
Climb 210m

A short walk into a stunning amphitheatre carved by ice to a summit with fine views

Start/finish	Layby on A470
Locate	///soda.warnings.downfield
Cafes/pubs	None on route
Transport	No public transport
Parking	Layby on A470 (LD3 8NH)
Toilets	No public toilets on route

This walk passes through the hollow of the cwm that is overshadowed by the steep craggy cliffs of Craig Cerrig-gleisiad. Early spring to mid-summer is the best time to see the wildflowers and excellent birdlife, while in August and September the mountain slopes are painted purple with heather. There is a relatively short but steep ascent to gain the summit of Fan Frynych and this is rewarded with a panoramic vista.

Aerial view of Craig Cerrig-gleisiad

SHORT WALKS BANNAU BRYCHEINIOG

WALK 4 – CRAIG CERRIG-GLEISIAD

Entrance to Craig Cerrig-gleisiad National Nature Reserve

1 Take the footpath to the right of the stream and follow this up into the cwm to a stone squeeze and a wooden gateway through the wall to a route marker.

> This area is part of a Graig Cerrig-gleisiad National Nature Reserve and packed full of wildlife. Rare alpine and Arctic-alpine plants that survived the last Ice Age inhabit the inaccessible gullies where they are just out of reach of grazing sheep.

2 This route follows the National Park's Bluestone Walk marked with the blue indicators. Continue straight ahead, climbing into the cwm with the path getting steeper before gaining the summit of **Fan Frynych**, marked by a trig point.

> The land on your right was once a Bronze Age settlement that was farmed 4000 years ago. In 2013 a stone was discovered here whose exposed face contained rock art: 12 cup marks joined by connecting lines.

3 Cross back to the path above the cwm and turn left, following the path with the cliff on your right to a junction of paths at **Twyn Dylluan-ddu**. The highest peaks in Southern Britain of Corn Du and Pen y Fan (886m) are visible across the valley.

4 Take the path that descends diagonally back across the slope into the cwm again. The small cliff on your right was formed by a landslide over which you cross. After just over 1.5km you will come to the route marker you encountered earlier on. Turn left, retracing your steps back to the start.

> ⓘ *The magnificent red kite is now a common sight in the national park, but by the 1980s it had been persecuted almost to extinction.*

The route through the cwm passes by botanically interesting boggy areas that contain extraordinary species such as the carnivorous sundew, which flowers between June and August. The rocks exposed in the main crag are Senni Beds of Devonian Old Red Sandstone, topped with Brownstones.

Purple saxifrage (Saxifraga oppositifolia) growing in a steep gulley in the nature reserve

WALK 4 – CRAIG CERRIG-GLEISIAD

View of Pen y Fan and Corn Du with the steep crags of Craig Cerrig-gleisiad on the right

– To shorten

Follow the red waymarked boot indicators to do the Under the Cliff Walk. This makes the route 1hr shorter and avoids the steep climb to the summit of Fan Frynych.

Glacial origins

It is believed that the cwm was occupied by a small glacier during the last period of glacial activity when small glaciers developed and perennial snow patches formed in the shadows of northern-facing scarps. This was the last cold period, which ended around 10,000 years ago. Persistent erosion of the western wall by glacial and freeze-thaw action led to slumping and rockfalls. The hummocky terrain left in the hollow was produced by the last small glacier, but some of it may have been left by the earlier Late Devensian ice sheet, which covered the entire Brecon Beacons around 20,000 years ago.

Bridge across the Blaen Taf Fawr at Pont ar daf

WALK 5
Pen y Fan

Time 3½hr
Distance 7.5km (4¾ miles)
Climb 500m

Challenge yourself to reach the highest summit in South Wales

Start/finish	*Pont ar Daf car park*
Locate	*///oblige.diagram.tweed*
Cafes/pubs	*None on route*
Transport	*On main bus route between Brecon and Merthyr Tydfil*
Parking	*National Trust car park at Pont ar Daf, or opposite Storey Arms Centre, or layby to the north (LD3 8NL)*
Toilets	*At Pont ar Daf car park*

This is the quickest route to the two highest peaks in the Beacons, Pen y Fan and Corn Du, and by far the most popular. Route finding is easy in good weather but conditions can change dramatically if the wind picks up and the cloud comes down. Temperatures drop with altitude, so make sure you are well equipped for this high excursion, the rewards of which include some of the best mountain views in Wales. Take care when approaching the north-facing cliff of Pen y Fan and Corn Du, as they both have precipitous drops.

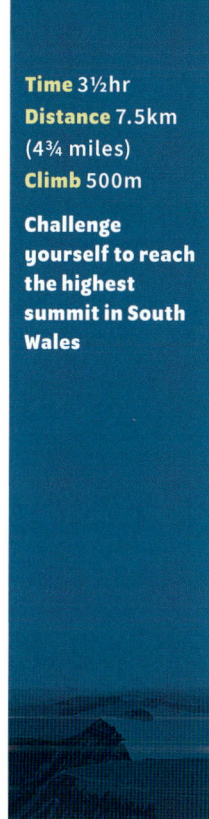

Iron Age cairn on the summit of Pen y Fan

SHORT WALKS BANNAU BRYCHEINIOG

1 Exit **Pont ar Daf** car park by taking the path across a bridge crossing **Blaen Taff Fawr** and follow the well-marked track for 2km up the hillside to **Bwlch Duwynt**.

2 Bear left at the col and take the path that follows the top of the crags, which then skirts across the slope below **Corn Du** and climbs up to the summit of **Pen y Fan**.

> You have reached the highest summit in southern Britain at 886m (2906ft). The cairn at the summit is a Bronze Age burial chamber and look out for ripple marks in some of the exposed rocks.

3 Retrace your steps off the summit, cross over the saddle and ascend **Corn Du**. Be careful of the steep drop off the northern cliff edge that drops into Cwm Llwch below. Corn Du (Black

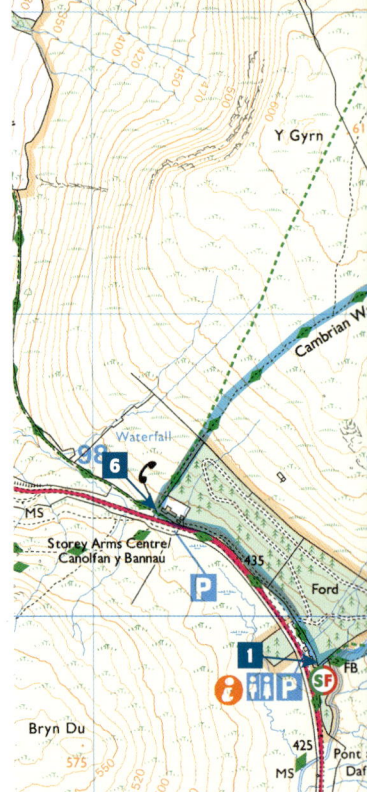

Path leading up to Bwlch Duwynt

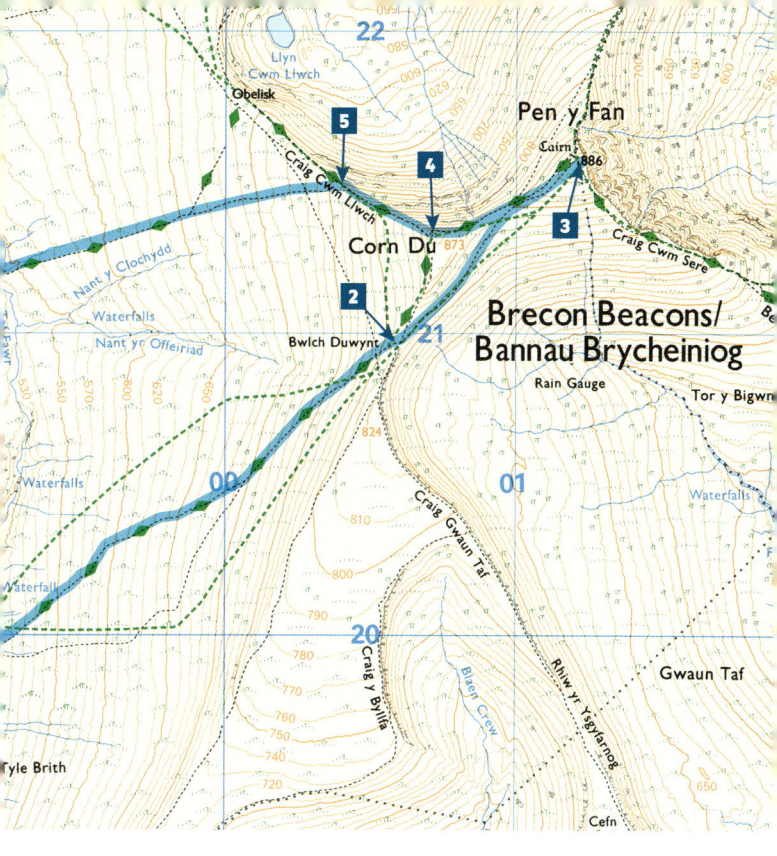

Horn) is the site of a Bronze Age cairn and the stones near the edge are the remains of an excavated funerary mound.

4 Continue in the same direction and descend a steep section to the ridge below and head along the ridge towards Tommy Jones' Obelisk with the glacial lake of Llyn Cwm Llwch visible at the head of the valley below.

The obelisk is a memorial to a young boy who died there in 1900.

5 Leave the ridge path where it divides before the obelisk and bear left on the footpath for just over 1km to cross the stream of **Blaen Taf Fawr** and then head down to join the A470 road by the distinctive red telephone box.

Summit of Corn Du with the path on the left leading to Bwlch Duwynt

6 Turn left and follow the path in front of the **Storey Arms Centre** and through a kissing gate to a track that takes you back to the start.

Telephone box where the path comes back to the Storey Arms

Pen y Fan vista

The summit of Pen y Fan is one of the finest vantage points in Wales. On an exceptionally clear day, Cadair Idris in the Eryri National Park (Snowdonia) can just be distinguished to the north and Exmoor to the south. Almost due west are the cliffs of a beautiful glacial cwm, Craig Cerrig-gleisiad, and beyond is Fforest Fawr, a relatively unvisited part of the park that possesses many interesting features. To the south-west, when there is good visibility, the wide sweep of Swansea Bay can be seen, which culminates in the west with the Mumbles Lighthouse.

WALK 6
Llyn Cwm Llwch

Start/finish	*Nant Cwm Llwch car park*
Locate	*///seashell.initial.atomic*
Cafes/pubs	*None on route*
Transport	*No public transport*
Parking	*Nant Cwm Llwch car park (LD3 8NE)*
Toilets	*No public toilets on route*

Time 2hr
Distance 8km (5 miles)
Climb 300m

A gradual climb to reach a magical lake that holds an enchanted island

This route takes you into the head of Cwm Llwch and to a mythical lake. There is then a steep climb to the ridge and to Tommy Jones' Obelisk and Pen Milan, with a more relaxed option just exploring the lake. This is crystal clear making it a great place for a wild swim but remember that the water will be chilly. An enchanted island may appear on May Day if you are lucky!

View of Twyn y Dyfnant from Cwm Llwch

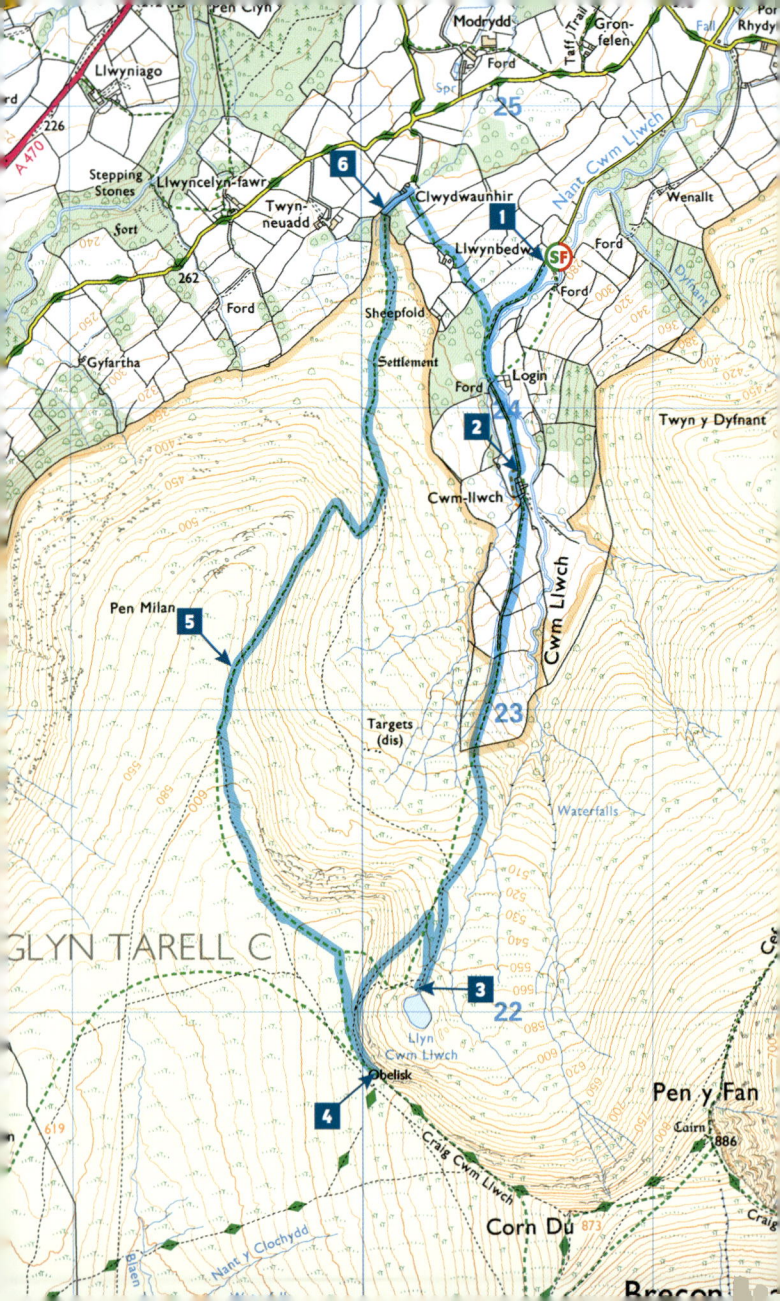

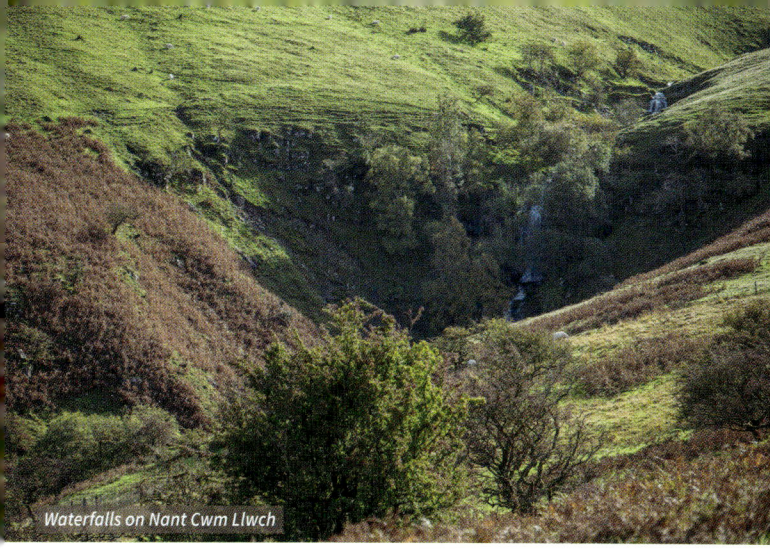
Waterfalls on Nant Cwm Llwch

1 Start at the end of the car park where there is a 'No Vehicles' sign with the stream **Nant Cwm Llwch** on your left. Follow the track leading into the valley to the cottage at **Cwm-llwch**, with Twyn y Dyfnant marking the end of the ridge of Cefn Cwm Llwch up on your left. The impressive headwall ahead is formed by Corn Du on the right and Pen y Fan on the left.

2 Follow the detour around the cottage and continue along the path that climbs steadily to the hill fence. It is worth making a detour to the left to explore the waterfalls in the two stream gullies as these are picturesque and full of wildlife. The route continues straight ahead to **Llyn Cwm Llwch**.

The lake, only 8m deep, was formed by a block of ice lingering on during the last Ice Age. Rock fragments were plucked from the crags above, accumulating in a ring and damming a small lake when the ice melted.

3 Take time to take in the wonderful atmosphere at the lake and then take the steep path to gain the ridge of Craig Cwm Llwch above and turn left to **Tommy Jones' Obelisk**.

The obelisk is a memorial to Tommy Jones, aged five, who died here in 1900 of exhaustion. He tragically became lost in the dark when trying to return to Login from the old farm at Cwm-llwch you passed earlier on.

Gorge section of Nant Cwm Llwch

> ⓘ *The Central Beacons massif was gifted by the Eagle Star Insurance Company in 1964 to the National Trust.*

4 Retrace your steps along the ridge and follow the footpath which swings first right, left, then right again around the head of a side valley of Cwm Llwch, with steep slopes on the right. The path changes into an old broad green quarry track just before the final spur of **Pen Milan**. This track was once used to transport Old Red Sandstone from an abandoned quarry on the left.

5 Descend the slope with the path becoming ill-defined in places but eventually the fences on either side funnel you to a gate.

6 Pass through the gate, ford a small stream and follow the tree-lined track to the yard with the cottage of **Clwydwaunhir** on the left. Opposite the house are a small ford and a stile. Cross these and cut across some fields to the track you used near the beginning of the route. Turn left and back to the start of the walk.

− To shorten

Retrace your steps back down the valley from Llyn Cwm Llwch, avoiding the steep climb to the ridge and reducing the distance to 2.5km (2hr).

Mythical Llyn Cwm Llwch

Legend has it that Llyn Cwm Llwch had an enchanted island, only accessible through a tunnel from the shore. The island would rise out of the water only on May Day, when visitors to the island would be presented with fairy flowers and enjoy enchanting fairy music. The flowers were so lovely that one sacrilegious visitor decided to take some away with him down the mountain. When they faded, the island disappeared below the waters and was never seen again.

Swimming in Llyn Cwm Llwch

Bridge across Nant Gwdi

WALK 7
Cwm Sere

Start/finish	*Cwm Gwdi car park*
Locate	*///herbs.coach.habits*
Cafes/pubs	*None on route*
Transport	*No public transport*
Parking	*Cwm Gwdi National Trust car park (LD3 8LE)*
Toilets	*No public toilets on route*

Time 2hr
Distance 5.5km (3½ miles)
Climb 115m

Venture into the amphitheatre formed by Cribyn and Pen y Fan, the most spectacular valley in the national park

This mostly level route brings you into the heart of the park and has a remote, wilderness feel, even though the summit of Pen y Fan might be swarming with people on the edge of the towering cliff that looms 500m above you at the end of the route. You can choose how far you wish to explore along the valley side up to the headwall, and the stream has many tumbling waterfalls and pools to swim in on a warm day. The path can be muddy in places so walking boots are recommended.

Allt Ddu

SHORT WALKS BANNAU BRYCHEINIOG

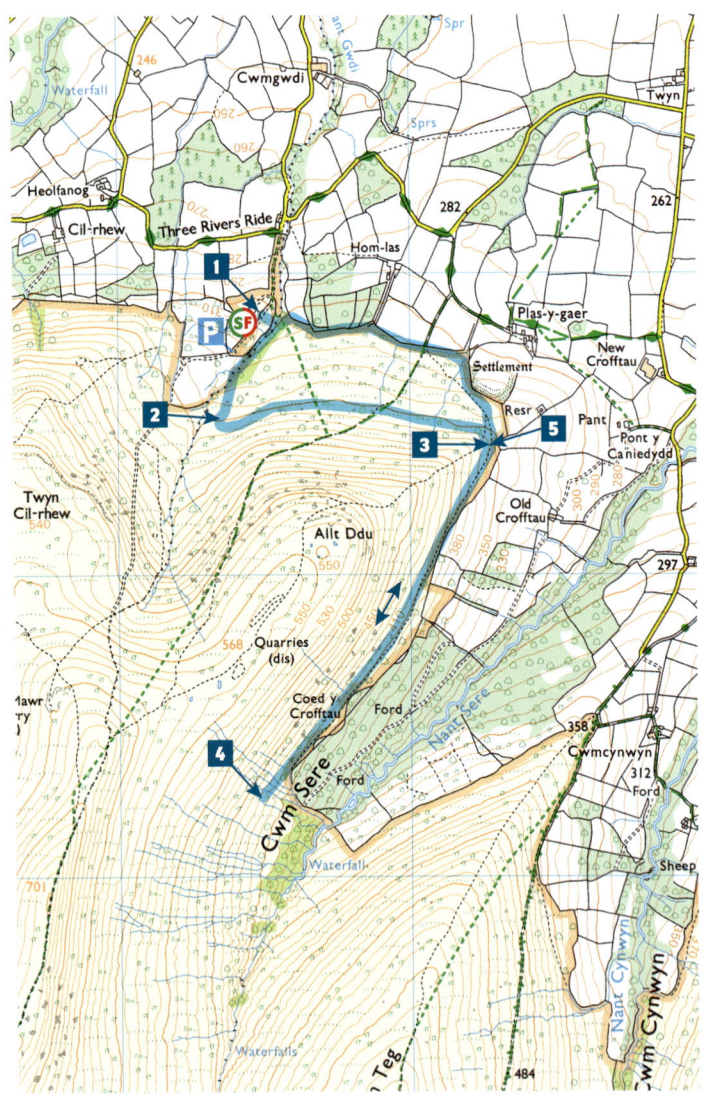

46

WALK 7 – CWM SERE

1 Take the footpath to the left of the ticket machine, ignoring the obvious route through the gate at the top of the car park, and descend into the stream gully of **Nant Gwdi**.

> Cwm Gwdi car park was once the site of an army training camp dating back to late Victorian times. The concrete bases of Nissen huts can still be seen and it was still in use until the 1990s.

> ⓘ *The slopes of Beacons valleys often have a high density of hawthorn trees, supporting bird species such as ring ouzel, redwing and fieldfare.*

Cross the bridge, climb out of the gulley and bear right at the top, keeping the stream on your right, through the woodland to the open hillside to meet a junction of paths. Keep a look out for fungi growing on trees, decaying wood or in the grass on woodland floor.

2 Turn left, with the hillside of **Allt Ddu** above on your right and follow the path that contours around the slope and into **Cwm Sere**.

> Cwm Sere was carved by ice into a U-shape, but this has been altered slightly by a snowbed eating away at its western side in post-glacial times and by Nant Sere eroding away a notch in its base.

Pen y Fan and Cribyn from the start of Cwm Sere

Aerial view of Cwm Sere in autumn

3 The path keeps level and gradually becomes less distinct beyond where the hill fence ends on your left. Carry on into the head of the valley for as far as you feel comfortable. The wood-lined stream of Nant Sere below has many waterfalls and pools and is worth exploring but don't forget that you will have to climb back up again!

4 When you are ready retrace your steps back down the valley to where the path bears left at the end of **Allt Ddu**.

5 Take the path along the fence that will lead you back to the bridge and car park, looking out for the impressive obvious ditch and tree-lined earth rampart at **Plas-y-gaer** on your right.

> ⓘ *Many of the high summits in the Bannau Brycheiniog National Park have Bronze Age burial cairns dating back to 2300–800BC.*

Plas-y-gaer is an Iron Age settlement some 2000 years old, *gaer* **meaning 'fortress' and** *plas* **meaning 'place'. The site is unexcavated but was probably built to defend the surrounding fertile land.**

North-east face of Pen y Fan

This imposing feature rises some 380m, becoming vertical near the top. The brown scars on the face of the mountain are testimony to the relentless onslaught of the elements and processes of erosion. The deadliest of these is the freezing and thawing of water in cracks in the rocks, which literally shatters the stone. The steep, impregnable face protects some of Britain's true botanical treasures from grazing sheep. The combination of high altitude and a shaded northern aspect creates living conditions more akin to polar latitudes than to temperate southern Britain. Ledges high up on the face are crammed full of interesting and unusual species such as purple saxifrage, an Arctic-alpine, that survived the last Ice Age.

Oak trees growing on the earth rampart of Plas-y-gaer Iron Age fort

Largest waterfall on Blaen-y-glyn

WALK 8
Blaen-y-glyn waterfalls

Start/finish	*Blaen-y-glyn Isaf car park*
Locate	*///fiery.manual.oppose*
Cafes/pubs	*None on route*
Transport	*No public transport*
Parking	*Blaen-y-glyn Isaf car park (CF48 2UT)*
Toilets	*No public toilets on route*

Time 1½hr
Distance 4km (2½ miles)
Climb 185m

The mesmerising roar of the tumbling Afon Caerfanell fills the gorge of Blaen-y-glyn

This walk climbs alongside the Afon Caerfanell as it plunges in a series of cascades from the glacial hanging valley above. There are numerous plunge pools to swim in on a warm day and plenty of wildlife to see. Spring months are a wonderful time to visit, with wildflowers and hawthorn trees in blossom. Autumn brings the rich warm palette of reds, yellows and oranges before leaves are shed for the winter. The terrain is easy at first with some uneven sections above the main fall.

Hanging valley part of Blaen-y-glyn

SHORT WALKS BANNAU BRYCHEINIOG

1 Exit the car park onto the road, turn left and cross the bridge over the **Afon Caerfanell**. Turn left off the road and follow the path along the bank of the river that flows down the Blaen-y-glyn valley ahead to a bridge.

Keep glancing at the stream bed for a chance to see the specialist bird of this habitat, the dipper. On a quiet day you are likely to chase a pair upstream until they reach the end of their territory.

2 Explore the waterfall just upstream by crossing over the bridge. The plunge pool is great for a refreshing dip on a warm day. Come back over the bridge and continue along the same bank as before, heading up the gorge to the hill fence.

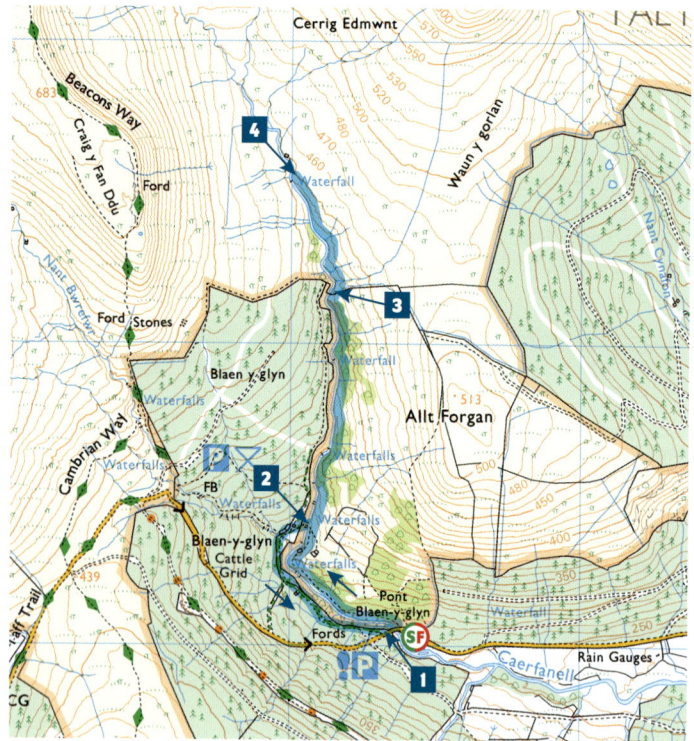

Upper wooded part of Blaen-y-glyn in autumn

> ⓘ Until a 1000 years ago Eurasian brown bears fed on berries and salmon in the national park and wolves hunted deer with their packs, disappearing sometime in the 18th century.

The flat surface of the large stone on your right above the hill fence has been inscribed 'GH' and the year '1845'. The initials may well be those of the Gwynne Halfords of Buckland, a large land-owning family in Victorian times.

3 Pass through the gate in the hill fence and continue along the path above the gorge to the final waterfall where the gradient flattens out. This marks the start of the hanging valley.

Ahead on the right is the slope of Cerrig Edmwnt leading up to Cwar y Gigfran. This crag was formed by a massive landslide that was caused by the stream undermining the stability of the valley side.

4 Retrace your steps back to the bridge. Cross over and take the path on the opposite bank of the river through the woodland back to the car park.

+ To lengthen

From Waypoint 4 continue following the Afon Caerfanell for as far as you wish.

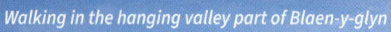
Walking in the hanging valley part of Blaen-y-glyn

Hanging valley

The upper half of Blaen-y-glyn has been left 'hanging' above the main Talybont Valley. During the Ice Age, Blaen-y-glyn would have contained a small glacier that fed the main glacier responsible for carving out the Talybont Valley. This glacier in turn fed one of the major glaciers that flowed down the Usk Valley. The stream that now drains the classically ice-sculpted, U-shaped hanging valley has cut a small 'V' notch in the valley floor and plunges over the overhang in a series of waterfalls.

Falls on the lower part of Baen-y-glyn in autumn

WALK 9
Pencelli canal walk

Start/finish	Layby on B4558 at Pencelli
Locate	///worth.sharpens.boater
Cafes/pubs	Pub and restaurant in Pencelli
Transport	Bus service from Brecon and Abergavenny stops in village, 200m from start
Parking	Layby on B4558 at Pencelli (LD3 7LX)
Toilets	No public toilets on route

Time 2½hr
Distance 9km (5½ miles)
Climb 20m

Take a stroll in the slow lane of the towpath, surrounded by wildlife

This walk couldn't be more relaxed as you follow the level towpath alongside the canal. Autumn is without doubt the prime time to visit as you wander under the trees with their reflection in the water reminiscent of a painting by Monet. There is plenty of wildlife along the route and you may see a canal boat as it glides serenely past.

Canal boats at the marina near Storehouse Bridge

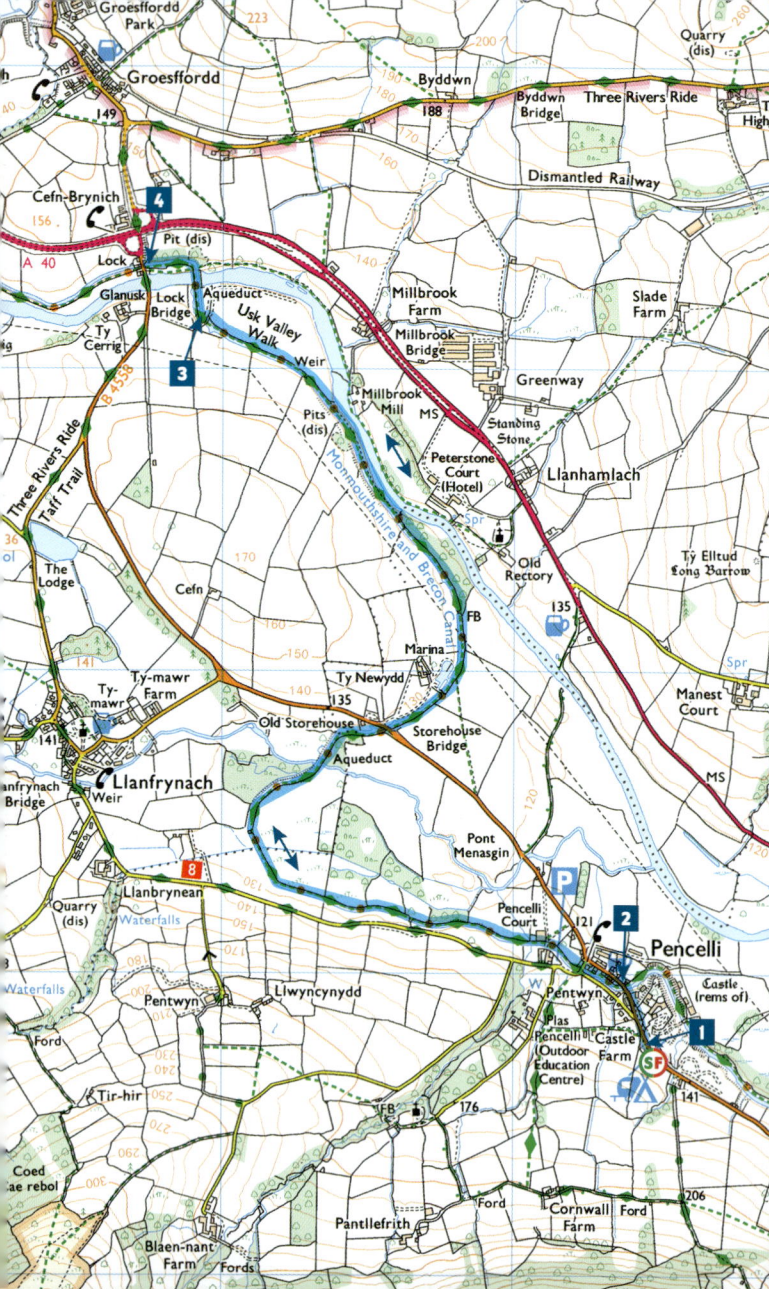

WALK 9 – PENCELLI CANAL WALK

1 Turn left out of the layby and along the grassy verge into the village, passing **Pencelli Castle** Caravan and Camping Site on your right to reach the road bridge over the canal.

The entrance to the caravan and camping park was once an impressive gatehouse and two towers. There is no public access to the remaining manor house that can be seen just afterwards.

2 Turn left just over the bridge and go down the steps to the towpath. Turn right and continue with the **Monmouthshire and Brecon Canal** on your left. The towpath crosses an aqueduct and goes past the Old Storehouse just before going under the B4558 at Storehouse Bridge. Continue for 4km until you reach

The Brynich Aqueduct seen from near the route

Bridge 162. The canal runs side-by-side with the River Usk for a while, and the elevated towpath gives great views of the rapids at the weir that supplied the water for Millbrook Mill on the opposite side of the river.

3 Cross over the canal bridge, following the signs for Brecon, and continue along the towpath over the River Usk on the **Brynich Aqueduct** and to Brynich Lock.

The canal crosses over the River Usk on the Brynich Aqueduct

Monmouthshire and Brecon Canal in autumn

> ⓘ *The Brynich Aqueduct carries the Monmouthshire and Brecon Canal over the River Usk. It was built in 1800 and restored in 1997.*

— To shorten

Just go along the towpath for as far as you wish.

+ To lengthen

Retrace your steps to Bridge 162 and cross over. Turn left and take the path over the aqueduct again (but now on the opposite bank) and turn right along the bank of the river. Continue along the River Usk for as far as you wish towards Peterstone Court Country House and the Church of St Peter and St Illtyd in Llanhamlach. Return to Bridge 162 and retrace your steps back to the start. This adds 4km (1hr) to your walk if you go as far as the church.

4 After exploring the picturesque lock, and perhaps having a break at the picnic tables, retrace your steps back to the start.

It is possible to canoe or paddleboard on the canal if you have a British Waterways Boat licence. These and narrowboats can be hired for the day at various locations.

Pencelli Castle

Pencelli Castle started as a fortified timber and earth structure built in the 1080s by a member of the Baskerville family as a reward for supporting Bernard de Neufmarché, one of William the Conqueror's knights. It was rebuilt in stone in the 13th century and was an impressive Norman castle with a gatehouse and two towers.

It became redundant as a fortification by the end of the 14th century and the stone was robbed for other buildings. The current Elizabethan manor house was built in 1583 from these stones and includes parts of St Leonard's Chapel that was situated inside the protective walls of the castle. The cellar was once a dungeon, and the shackles and chains are now held in the National Museum of Wales in Cardiff.

Narrowboat near the Ashford Tunnel

WALK 10
Canal, Usk Valley and Afon Caerfanell

Start/finish	*Lifting bridge in Talybont-on-Usk*
Locate	*///croak.salt.headstone*
Cafes/pubs	*Pubs in Talybont-on-Usk*
Transport	*Bus service from Brecon and Abergavenny*
Parking	*On street in Talybont-on-Usk*
Toilets	*At Henderson Hall (100m from bridge)*

Time 2½hr
Distance 9km (5½ miles)
Climb 170m

Tranquillity and wildlife on a leisurely walk along a river and canal

This walk starts with the peace and quiet of the canal towpath and finishes with a scenic section of the Afon Caerfanell. The middle part of the walk climbs out of the Usk Valley to a fantastic viewpoint of the Caerfanell Valley and the highest mountains in Bannau Brycheiniog beyond. The area has a rich industrial past that explains the numerous pubs in Talybont-on-Usk with gardens overlooking the canal.

Afon Caerfanell in autumn

WALK 10 – CANAL, USK VALLEY AND AFON CAERFANELL

1 Park on the road in the village near to the lifting bridge which is the start of the walk. Turn left at the bridge and follow the canal towpath through the village to the stone and metal bridges behind the White Hart pub.

Lime kilns at Talybont-on-Usk

The first (stone) bridge leads to the Brinore Tramroad, while the Brecon and Merthyr Railway ran over the second (metal) bridge. Crushed limestone and coal were burnt in the bank of limekilns to make quicklime. This was packed in barrels and transported by canal barge.

2 Continue along the route for 3km to Bridge 138, passing some lime kilns on the right just before the next stone road bridge. One section takes to the road when the canal enters the 200m long **Ashford Tunnel**. When the road starts to descend, pick up a footpath on the right of the road by the turning to Ashford Cottage and this becomes the towpath once again at the end of the tunnel. Canal boats were usually 'legged' through tunnels by two boatmen, but notches in the roof of this tunnel suggest that poles were used here.

Boat emerging from Ashford Tunnel

63

Monmouthshire and Brecon Canal at Talybont-on-Usk

The canal was once a busy industrial route carrying limestone, iron ore and coal. Narrow boats, canoes and stand-up paddleboards now ply its tranquil navigation for some 36 miles. It is regarded as one of the most picturesque canals in the UK.

3 Go under Bridge 138 and turn left up the steps, signposted for Llanddetty Church. Turn left over the canal bridge and bear right on the **Usk Valley Walk** that crosses the fields diagonally uphill to meet a road. Bear right and walk a short distance down to the cattle grid.

4 Leave the road by turning left onto footpath just before the cattle grid. Cross the field along the hedge on the right at first and then contour around the hill and descend the fields diagonally left to meet a bridleway that was once the Brinore Tramroad. Ahead is a fantastic view of the central Beacons with Talybont Reservoir in the valley below.

5 Turn right, still on the Usk Valley Trail for just under 2km to where the trail turns left.

> ⓘ *Five out the six locks on the Monmouthshire and Brecon Canal are found at Llangynidr. They raise the level of the canal by around 17m.*

WALK 10 – CANAL, USK VALLEY AND AFON CAERFANELL

6 Turn left, signposted Usk Valley Trail, and descend, crossing the dismantled railway to reach the footbridge across the **Afon Caerfanell**. This was once the course of the Brecon and Merthyr Tydfil Junction Railway and connected Dowlais with Brecon. Cross the bridge, then turn right and follow the footpath through the fields with the river on your right. The path veers away from the river to meet the road.

The path through the fields is part of the Henry Vaughan Trail. Henry Vaughan (1621–95) was a poet and doctor who, with his twin brother Thomas, was born at Newton Farm. He was known as 'The Swan of Usk'.

7 Turn right and follow the road back to the lifting bridge and the start.

Brinore Tramroad

The Brinore Tramroad was a primitive 8-mile horse-drawn railway, operating between 1815 and 1865, that brought limestone down from Trefil Quarries. The stone was loaded into barges and shipped east via the canal to Tredegar Ironworks. The gauge was 3ft 4in and it was the L-shaped cast-iron rails that guided the wheels on the trams that had no flange. The trams weighed half a ton when empty, with heaviest loads of 2¼ tons carried by 1835. One horse could pull a loaded tram on the flat and bring an empty one back up the incline from Talybont. A replica tram and more history can be seen in Talybont-on-Usk.

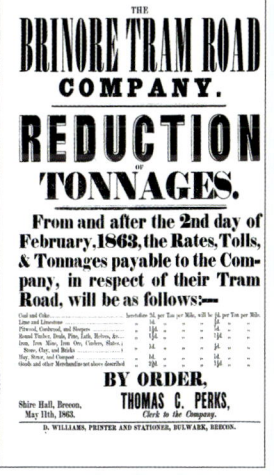

Brinore Tramroad tariffs from 1863

Boats at Llangynidr

WALK 11
River Usk, canal and Llangynidr Bridge

Time 2¼hr
Distance 7.5km (4¾ miles)
Climb 45m

A beautiful river and canal are your companions on this level walk in the Usk Valley

Start/finish	Coach and Horses pub in Llangynidr
Locate	///tenses.linguists.punchy
Cafes/pubs	Pub and store in Llangynidr
Transport	Bus service from Abergavenny and Brecon stops at Llangynidr village hall
Parking	Coach and Horses pub car park in Llangynidr (NP8 1LS)
Toilets	No public toilets on route

Based on the village of Llangynidr, this walk visits one of most picturesque stretches of the River Usk with some spectacular rapids. The path runs close to the water's edge, so this route may not be possible if the river level is high. The Monmouthshire and Brecon Canal provides a tranquil counterpoint to the energy of the rushing river water. The River Usk is a famed trout fishery with opportunities to buy a day ticket.

Monmouthshire and Brecon Canal at Llangynidr

SHORT WALKS BANNAU BRYCHEINIOG

1 Turn right out of the pub car park and cross the bridge over the canal. Turn left on to the towpath and left again back under the road with the canal on your right. Continue for a little over 3km to Bridge 125.

> As you walk alongside the canal look out for kingfisher, swan, coot, heron and moorhen, together with colourful dragonflies and damselflies. The colourful mandarin duck has also become established here.

2 Leave the towpath just before Bridge 125 and take the footpath which drops down into the stream gully and over the bridge. Follow this past **Dyfnant** down to the bank of the River Usk. Turn left and follow the bank with the river on your right to join a road at a bridge over the Nant Cleister.

> The River Usk was once regarded as being one of the finest salmon rivers in Wales and one of the best trout rivers in the UK. Large trout up to five pounds have been caught. Salmon numbers are now sadly a fraction of what they once were.

Salmon waiting to spawn in the winter

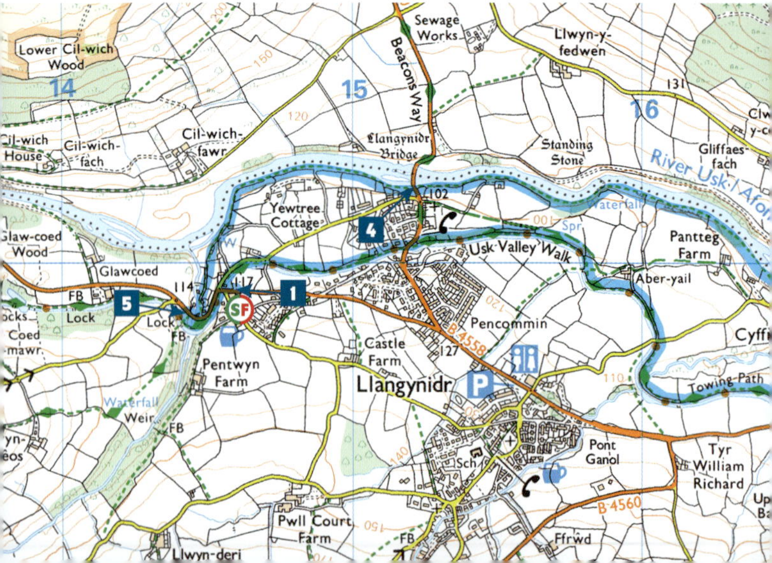

WALK 11 – RIVER USK, CANAL AND LLANGYNIDR BRIDGE

Bridge at Llangynidr

3 Turn right and continue along the road past **Cyffredyn**. After 200m turn right down the track back to the riverbank and follow the footpath with the river again on your right to **Llangynidr Bridge**. There is an option to shorten the walk here.

Llangynidr Bridge is an impressive structure and is the oldest bridge on the River Usk. It was built in 1706 and has six arches. It originally carried horse and carts, and the V cuts acted as refuges for pedestrians to stand to allow them to pass.

4 Cross over the road and continue along the river. The path is diverted away from the **River Usk** when it meets the Afon Crawnnon and this brings you to the road. Turn right, cross over the river and turn left and up the steps to reach the canal towpath at a **lock**.

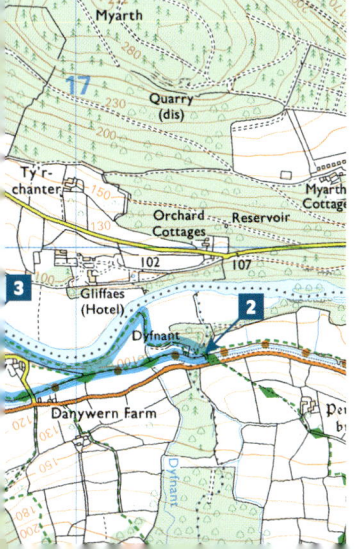

Three locks at Llangynidr

5 Turn left and follow the towpath with the canal on your right. Leave the towpath just before the road bridge in **Llangynidr** where you joined at the start of the walk. Cross the bridge and back to the pub.

> ### ✚ To lengthen
> Turn right at Waypoint 5 and go along the towpath for 1km to a staircase of three locks, then retrace your steps to continue the walk. Or follow the canal towpath west or east to make the walk as long as you wish.

Canal history

The Monmouthshire and Brecon Canal is navigable for around 36 miles from Brecon to Five Locks in Cwmbran. It dates to 1792 when an Act of Parliament created the Company of Proprietors of the Monmouthshire Canal Navigation allowing it to raise money for its construction. It was originally two separate canals with the Monmouthshire Canal opening in 1799 connecting Newport with Nantymoile Basin.

The Brecknock and Abergavenny Canal was built in 1812 extending the trade link from Pontymoile to Brecon. Both were abandoned in 1962, but the Brecknock and Abergavenny section and a small part of the Monmouthshire were reopened in 1970.

WALK 12
Craig y Cilau

Start/finish	*Llangattock Quarry car park*
Locate	*///reap.query.greet*
Cafes/pubs	*None on route*
Transport	*No public transport*
Parking	*Llangattock Quarry car park (NP8 1LG)*
Toilets	*No public toilets on route*

Time 2hr
Distance 7km (4¼ miles)
Climb 140m

A fascinating walk through a once-busy limestone quarry where nature now reigns

Craig y Cilau National Nature Reserve, designated for its rich limestone plant life, is one of the national park's rich treasures. Once a quarry, the area is now a caver's paradise, with an entrance to the famous Ogof Agen Allwedd system. This walk follows a level terrace cut into the escarpment as a tramroad. The circular route involves a steepish climb back up to the tramroad, but this can be avoided by taking the shorter out-and-back option. There are wonderful views of the Usk Valley.

Craig y Cilau and Cwm Onneu

Mossy saxifrage growing in Craig y Cilau National Nature Reserve

1 Leave the car park on a track and turn left after a short distance on a path heading straight up the slope to reach a level disused tramroad under the quarried cliff.

2 Turn right and continue following the tramroad through numerous spoil heaps and then turn left between two banks. Continue beneath the worked face of the old quarry at **Darren Cilau** and then drop down to rejoin the flat tramway.

> Look out for mossy saxifrage here in the spring and summer time. It is a white flower with four petals and is just one of the rare plants that grow on the lime-rich soil.

3 Continue along the terrace underneath **Chwar Mawr**, pausing to read the information board at the entrance to Craig y Cilau National Nature Reserve. Climb a short distance to a

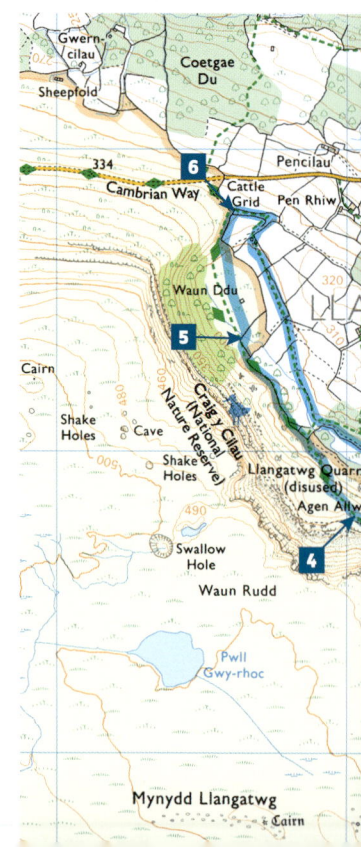

WALK 12 – CRAIG Y CILAU

cave entrance at the bend in the tramway at **Eglwys Faen**. Drop down to the terrace track again and continue along the base of the cliff.

The limestone cliffs are peppered with caves and Mynydd Llangattock contains extensive cave systems, including Ogof Agen Allwedd, with an impressive 37.5km of explored passageway.

It is an important winter roost for lesser horseshoe bats.

> ⓘ *Straight-tusked elephants, narrow-nosed rhinoceros, spotted hyenas and lions once roamed the mountains and valleys of the national park, with hippopotamus living in the River Usk 130,000 years ago.*

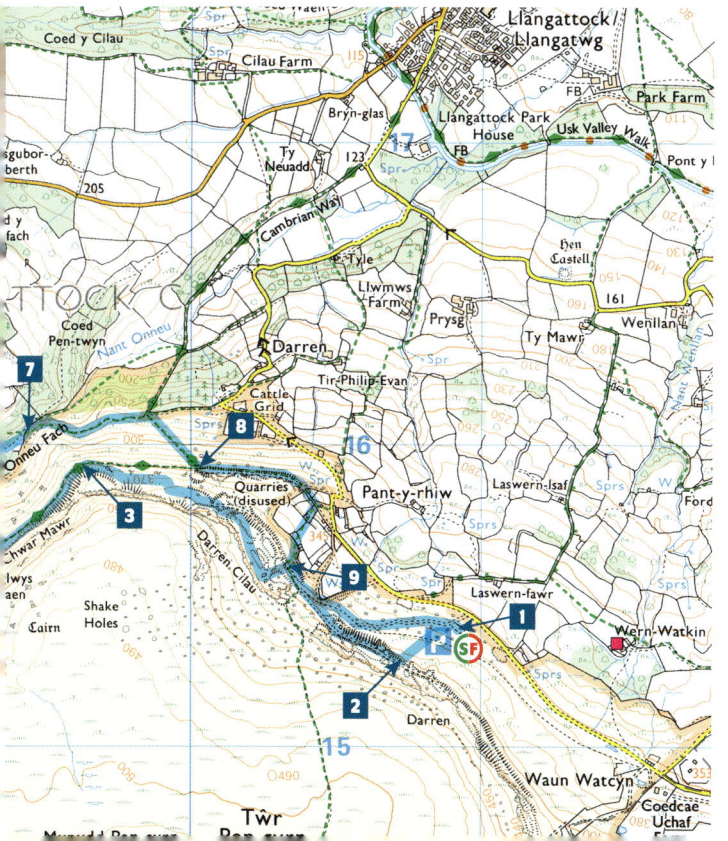

Bluebells and the quarried cliffs of Chwar Mawr

4 Turn right at a yellow fingerpost, taking the path that drops down across the valley side and take this to the edge of an obvious dome of the raised bog of Waun Ddu. Another option is to continue along the tramway for 330m to discover a gated entrance to Ogof Gam, the regular entrance to the Agen Allwedd cave system, and then return to the fingerpost.

5 Cross the stream by the collapsed stone wall and cross over **Waun Ddu** to two information boards and up to a farm track. Waun Ddu is a small, raised bog with species that are at home in acidic conditions. Look out for the carnivorous round-leaved sundew and bog pimpernel.

6 Turn right onto the farm track and take the next footpath on the right, which crosses the fields and drops down into **Cwm Onneu** to a fingerpost with two arrows. Bear left on the path that follows the Nant Onneu stream on your right, with the wood of **Coed Dyffryn** on your left.

The woodland and fields are spectacular in spring with a carpet of bluebells and a wonderful floral aroma. The woodland is also special and has four species of whitebeam, two of which are only known to grow in this area.

7 At the next fingerpost with a choice of two arrows, turn right and cross the stream over some stepping stones and

The raised bog of Waun Ddu

climb out of the valley to the next fingerpost. Take the path on the right that climbs steeply up to reach the tramway.

8 Turn left and follow the tramway, passing an old quarrymen's cottage. Shortly after, leave the trackway by turning right on a footpath that crosses up through the fields to another tramway.

9 Turn left and follow this tramway back to the start.

> **− To shorten**
>
> Continue along the level tramroad until the path descends then retrace your route to the start, to avoid a steep climb on the circular route.

Walking through Coed Dyffryn

Craig y Cilau National Nature Reserve

The quarried limestone cliffs of Chwar Mawr

In the 18th and 19th centuries this was a busy limestone quarry. The stone was taken by tram to the Monmouthshire and Brecon Canal in the valley below. The rock was processed into quicklime which was used as fertiliser, mortar and whitewash on stone buildings and as an essential ingredient in the manufacture of iron.

The area has now been reclaimed by wildlife and is one of Wales' most outstanding botanical sites, with over 250 species. One reason for this is the lime-rich soils that have allowed many rare plants and trees to thrive. Around 40 bird species have been recorded here, including ring ouzels: a migrant thrush that resembles a blackbird with a white bib.

Pen Cerrig-calch from Table Mountain

WALK 13
Table Mountain

Start/finish	Crickhowell Primary School car park
Locate	///small.hotspot.swooned
Cafes/pubs	Plenty of choice in Crickhowell
Transport	Bus service from Brecon to Abergavenny stops in Crickhowell
Parking	Park at school outside of school hours (NP8 1DY), or in nearby residential area
Toilets	At Crickhowell Community Sports Centre (400m off route)

Time 2hr
Distance 6km (3¾ miles)
Climb 360m

Height is steadily gained to reach the summit of Table Mountain with its magnificent panorama

Table Mountain is a striking mountain feature overlooking the town of Crickhowell that will tempt you to gain its viewpoint from the moment you arrive in the valley. The ascent begins with a picturesque walk alongside the wooded Cumbeth Brook, which is full of wildlife. A traverse across the mountainside brings you to the ancient site of Crug Hywel Fort and a chance to savour the magnificent views up and down the Usk Valley.

Bridge across the River Usk at Crickhowell

SHORT WALKS BANNAU BRYCHEINIOG

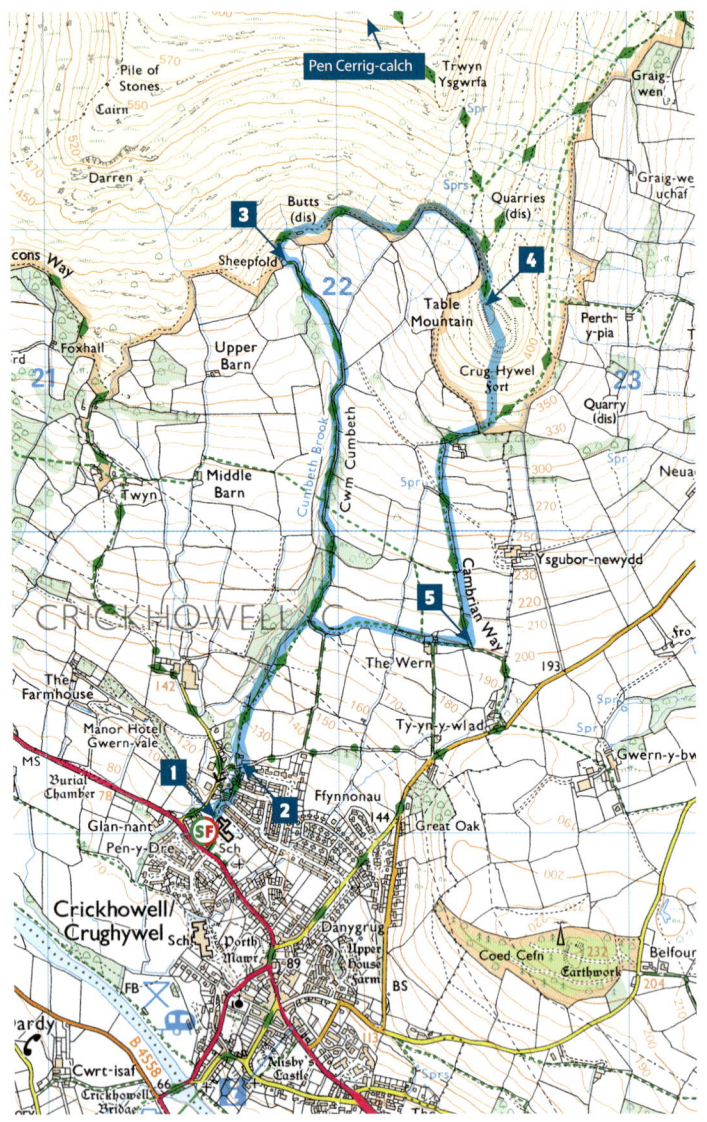

WALK 13 – TABLE MOUNTAIN

The famous Bear Hotel in Crickhowell near to start of walk

Crickhowell developed as a border town when the Normans built a motte and bailey castle in 1121. It was reinforced with stone in 1242 and again in 1400 but was sacked by Owain Glyndŵr in the early 15th century.

1 Walk up the road from the school car park and turn left up a narrow passageway after the second house, just past the apex of the bend. Cross over the next road on the path between the houses, go straight over again and turn left by the metal gate.

2 Turn right immediately on the path that runs along the stream, with Cumbeth Brook on your left, and follow **Cwm Cumbeth** for 2km to the hill fence.

3 Turn right and take the path along the fence. Climb up to gain the flat summit of Table Mountain and enjoy the commanding views from the top. The ditches and ruined stone defences are clear signs of how Iron Age man modified this hilltop to be the once formidable stronghold of Crug Hywel Fort.

4 Continue along the edge above the crags on your right and descend the steps at the end. Drop down to the path below on the right and follow it to the hill fence where the two drystone walls meet. Cross the stile and follow the path, which then turns to the left and drops down the slope through the fields.

5 Turn right on a footpath that leaves the path in the field just below the farm of **Ysgubor-newydd** and contour along the slope, passing the buildings at **The Wern** to rejoin the path along Cumbeth Brook. Turn left and retrace your steps back to the start.

> **+ To lengthen**
>
> Take the path up from Table Mountain to the summit of Pen Cerrig-calch where there even better views. This will add 7km (2hr) and 262m of sustained climbing.

Table Mountain

Table Mountain from Crickhowell

Formed by the dip slope of the resistant sandstone rocks, Table Mountain is the impressive setting for Crug Hywel, an Iron Age hill fort whose extensive ditches and ruined stone defences can still be seen today. It is possibly named after a local chieftain or after Hywel Dda, a well-respected prince of South Wales in the 10th century. Hywel introduced the Law of Wales, a set of social rules to free the common man from oppression by the upper classes. Crug Hywel means 'Hywel's Rock' in English and gives the town of Crickhowell its name.

WALK 14
Sugar Loaf

Start/finish	*Road end north of Abergavenny*
Locate	*///throats.doped.dreamers*
Cafes/pubs	*None on route*
Transport	*No public transport*
Parking	*Parking area at end of road north of Abergavenny (NP7 7HU)*
Toilets	*No public toilets on route*

Time 3hr
Distance 8km (5 miles)
Climb 420m

A sustained climb to reach a peak that stands on its own with a memorable 360-degree panorama

Sugar Loaf is an iconic mountain that stands alone in the Usk Valley. This walk gradually gains height through the stunning beech woodland that coats the slopes of St Mary's Vale. A sustained steepening climb brings you to the summit with its exceptional panoramic views. The return path is wonderfully open along the Rholben ridge, giving fantastic views of the Usk Valley. The stone bridge across Nant Iago near the beginning may be submerged after heavy rain, in which case you may want to leave the walk for another day.

The distinctive conical peak of the Sugar Loaf

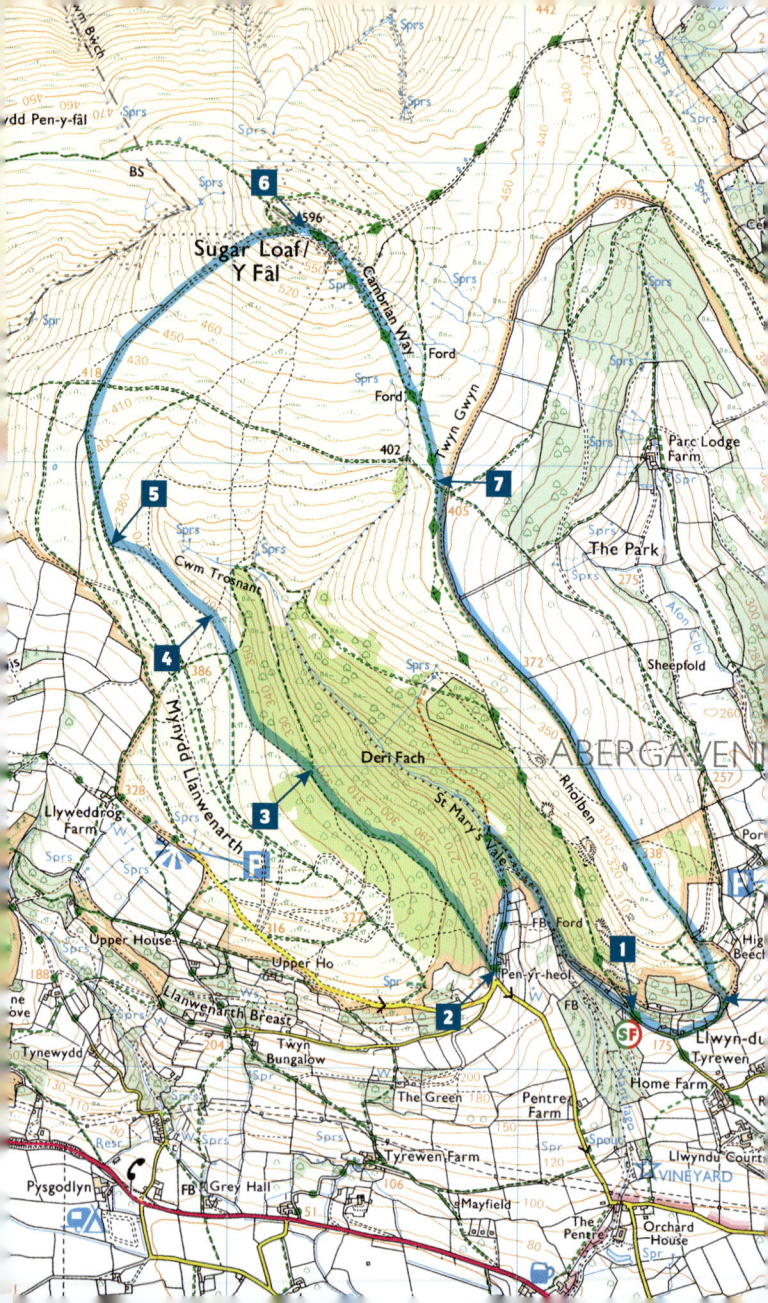

WALK 14 – SUGAR LOAF

1 Turn left from the car parking area and continue along the road, which becomes a track into the woodland of **Deri Fach** (Little Oaks) at the start of the valley of St Mary's Vale.

The wood is part of the Sugar Loaf Woodlands Site of Special Scientific Interest. The old sessile oak woodland is the largest example of its type and is near the south-eastern fringe of the habitat's range in UK and Europe.

Old sessile oak woodland in Deri Fach

Where it turns left back on itself by the side of the stream, climb diagonally across the slope through the beech woodland to a road and on to **Pen-yr-heol**.

2 Take the footpath back up to the right and ascend the sunken path through the wood. Bear right at a fork, ignoring the path that climbs on the left, and continue along the sunken track in the same direction, steadily climbing the side of the valley to reach another fork after just over 600m. *Look out for fungi that thrive in this habitat.*

3 Bear left at the fork and again keep steadily climbing, ignoring the path that descends the valley side, to emerge on to a grassy path that meets a junction of paths.

4 Continue straight across onto a narrower path if the bracken has not smothered it. *Otherwise, turn left and climb to the top of the ridge to meet a major path where you turn right.* Bear left at the next junction and continue climbing to the main path.

Trooping funnel mushroom in St Mary's Vale

SHORT WALKS BANNAU BRYCHEINIOG

5 Turn right, heading for the ridge ahead, ignoring the path that leaves on the right (this is the shortcut), to the next junction. Continue straight ahead up the sustained climb which progressively steepens to the trig point on the summit of the **Sugar Loaf**.

Mountains are sometimes called 'Sugar Loaf' when their shape resembles the conical mounds known as 'sugar loaves' that were formed by sugar being stored in piles after being extracted from sugar cane in Brazil.

6 Continue along the flat summit and descend the path along the **Cambrian Way** that leaves on your right and then descends parallel to a stream that emerges from a spring to reach a junction of paths at **Twyn Gwyn** (White Thread).

7 Continue straight ahead and then bear left to follow the path along the hill fence on your left. The Cibi Valley down to your left was once a medieval monastic deer park. It belonged to the Benedictine priory at Abergavenny. Keep straight ahead along the top of the **Rholben** ridge for about 1.5km, ignoring paths that leave on both sides, and then descend steeply straight down the nose to a gate in the hill fence.

8 Turn right and join the road to the junction with the road you drove up before. Turn right and walk up the road back to the start.

Nant Iago in St Mary's Vale

WALK 14 – SUGAR LOAF

> **– To shorten**
> To avoid the steep climb to the summit, after Waypoint 5 take the path on the right that runs across the slope to rejoin the route at Twyn Gwyn (Waypoint 7). This saves around 50min and 180m of ascent.

Sugar Loaf

View north to the Black Mountains from the summit of the Sugar Loaf

Sugar Loaf is commonly mistaken as being an extinct volcano. It is in fact composed of Old Red Sandstone, the sedimentary rock that forms much of the Black Mountains. The summit is made of quartz conglomerate, a very hard white rock, that has resisted erosion over millennia. It stands on its own due to the Usk glacier dividing around it as it travelled eastwards. The mountain was gifted to the National Trust by the suffragette Lady Rhondda.

The impressive 360-degree panoramic views from the summit are of the central Beacons summits to the west, Black Mountains to the north, Cotswolds and Skirrid Fawr to the east, and the Usk Valley to the south.

Start of the ascent to the summit of Ysgyryd Fawr

WALK 15
Ysgyryd Fawr (Skirrid Mountain)

Time 2hr
Distance 5km (3 miles)
Climb 335m

Wonderful views await as a reward for your efforts in summitting the 'shattered' mountain

Start/finish	The Skirrid National Trust car park on B4521
Locate	///marching.football.extremely
Cafes/pubs	Copper Kettle Tea Room (150m off route)
Transport	No public transport
Parking	National Trust car park (NP7 8AP)
Toilets	No public toilets on route

Standing separate from the rest of the mountains in the park, the Skirrid is a prominent landmark for miles around. Its Welsh name is Ysgyryd Fawr, meaning the 'Big Shattered' mountain. A relaxing woodland section leads you to the base of a steep climb to gain the summit with fine views. The gently sloping ridge brings you to a steep descent and back through the woodland to the start. The steep ascent to the summit and the descent at the end of the ridge can be avoided by carrying along the main path around the base of the mountain.

Rocky scar left by the landslide on the northern end of Ysgyryd Fawr

SHORT WALKS BANNAU BRYCHEINIOG

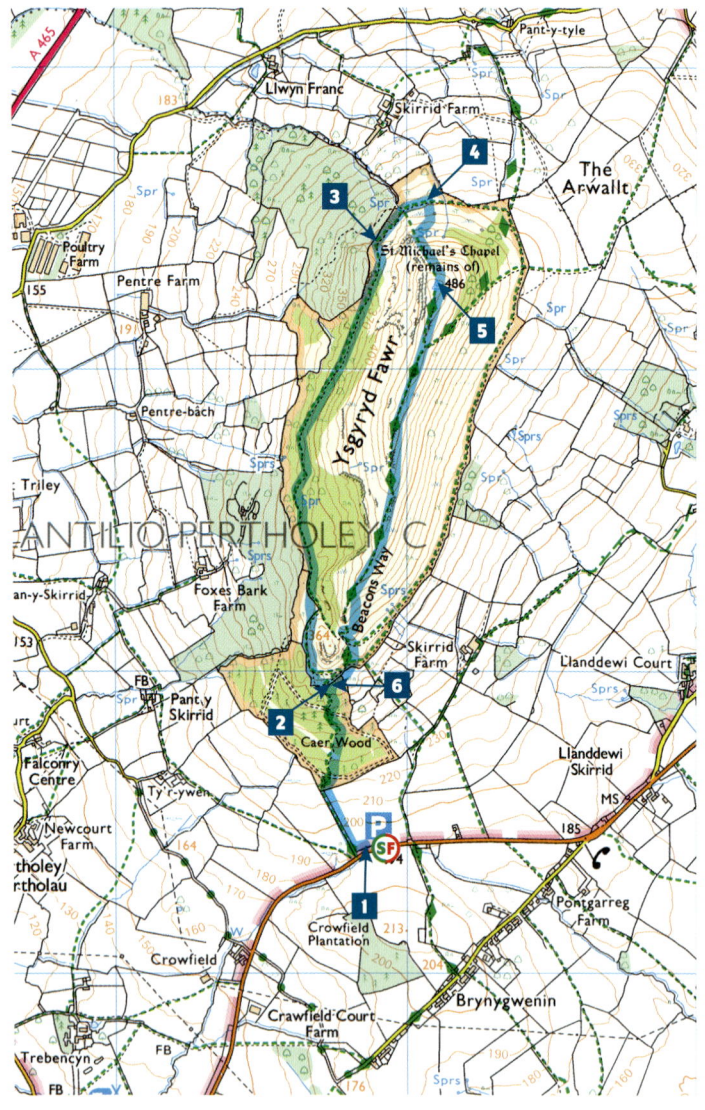

WALK 15 – YSGYRYD FAWR (SKIRRID MOUNTAIN)

1 With the road on your left, exit the car park at the end and turn right, following the signposted footpath to a swing gate at the start of **Caer Wood**. Continue climbing through the woodland, crossing over two tracks to reach a second swing gate.

2 Turn left along the path that skirts around the end of Ysgyryd Fawr, up above on your right. Follow this path through the woodland for a little over 1.5km, which has beautiful patches of bluebells in the springtime, to reach a large solitary boulder on the path. This marks where the end of the mountain up above collapsed in a landslide, leaving behind some impressive crags.

3 Just after this the route comes to a high point, with the crags above you near the end of the ridge and the mound on your left the remains of the landslide. Look and listen for peregrine falcons here. The path descends and rounds the end of the mountain.

Ysgyryd means 'trembling' or 'shaking' in Welsh and this gives a clue to the mountain's past. The crags and rock-strewn slope beneath are where the landslide occurred that gave rise to the mountain's name.

4 Look out for a small path on the right that climbs steeply along the cragline to the summit of **Ysgyryd Fawr**.

Walking through the bluebell woodland on the western flank of Ysgyryd Fawr

SHORT WALKS BANNAU BRYCHEINIOG

This may be slippery in wet conditions and if you prefer there is a slightly less steep route to the top which can be found by skirting further round to join the Beacons Way. The trig point is at an altitude of 486m and you may well be out of breath so take a break and appreciate the wonderful panorama.

Look out for the remains of St Michael's Chapel in the form of low banks, two entrance stones and a small kidney-shaped earthwork that was situated within a large prehistoric hill fort. The chapel was used by Roman Catholics during and after the Reformation, with services being held until at least 1680.

5 Proceed along the sloping ridge, joining the Beacons Way, and leave the ridge path towards the end down to the left and around the final promontory to the beginning of **Caer Wood** and the swing gate you passed through earlier. This promontory at the end of the mountain was once an Iron Age hill fort.

6 Retrace your steps back to the start.

View south along the ridge of Ysgyryd Fawr

WALK 15 – YSGYRYD FAWR (SKIRRID MOUNTAIN)

Skirrid Mountain Inn – the oldest pub in Wales

The Skirrid Mountain Inn

To the north of Ysgyryd Fawr in Llanvihangel Crucorney is the Skirrid Mountain Inn. Reputedly the first record for the inn is its use between 1100 and 1485 with a courtroom on the first floor. It is believed that around 183 hangings took place between the 12th and 17th centuries. The rope was suspended by the beam across the joist over the staircase. Owain Glyndŵr is said to have rallied his forces in the cobbled courtyard in the early 1400s.

Not surprisingly, the pub claims to be home to many ghosts, including the infamous Master Bloody Hangman Judge Jeffreys (1644–1689) who possibly sat in judgement here. He can be encountered on the stairs along with some of his victims who were laid out on the stone slab below the first step.

USEFUL INFORMATION

Tourism bodies

Brecon Beacons National Park www.breconbeacons.org
Visit Wales www.visitwales.com
The National Trust www.nationaltrust.org.uk
CADW cadw.gov.wales/visit/places-to-visit

Tourist information

Bannau Brycheiniog National Park Visitor Centre, Libanus, tel 01874 623366
Visit Brecon, Brecon, tel 01874 620860
Crickhowell Resource & Information Centre, Crickhowell, tel 01873 811970
Visit Abergavenny www.visitabergavenny.co.uk
Visit Brecon visitbrecon.org
Visit Crickhowell visitcrickhowell.wales
Visit Merthyr www.visitmerthyr.co.uk

Travel

Bus and train services:

Traws Cymru traws.cymru/en/services
www.breconbeacons.org/discover/getting-here/buses-and-trains
Traveline Cymru www.traveline.cymru
Stagecoach www.stagecoachbus.com

Attractions

Abergavenny Museum and Castle www.monlife.co.uk/heritage
Big Pit National Coal Museum https://museum.wales/bigpit

USEFUL INFORMATION

Blaenavon Ironworks www.visitblaenavon.co.uk/en/visit-blaenavon/places-to-visit

Craig-y-Nos Country Park https://bannau.wales/planning/heritage2/heritage-hotspots

Cyfarthfa Park & Castle www.visitmerthyr.co.uk/things-to-do/attractions

Dan-yr-Ogof – The National Showcaves Centre for Wales www.showcaves.co.uk

Goytre Wharf & Canal Visitor Centre www.goytrewharf.com

Llanthony Priory https://cadw.gov.wales/visit/places-to-visit/llanthony-priory

The Brecon Mountain Railway www.bmr.wales

Weather

Mountain weather forecast www.metoffice.gov.uk/weather/specialist-forecasts/mountain

Wind forecast www.windy.com

Met Office www.metoffice.gov.uk

© Andy Davies 2025
First edition 2025
ISBN: 978 1 78631 235 8
eISBN: 978 1 78765 178 4

Printed in Singapore by KHL Printing on responsibly sourced paper.
A catalogue record for this book is available from the British Library.
All photographs are by the author unless otherwise stated.
Cover illustration of Pen y Fan by Avery Mitchell.

© Crown copyright and database rights 2025 OS AC0000810376

Cicerone's EU representative for GPSR compliance is Easy Access System Europe, Mustamäe tee 50, 10621 Tallinn, Estonia. Email gpsr.requests@easproject.com.

CICERONE

Cicerone Press, Juniper House, Murley Moss, Oxenholme Road,
Kendal, Cumbria, LA9 7RL

www.cicerone.co.uk

Updates to this Guide

While every effort is made to ensure the accuracy of guidebooks as they go to print, changes can occur during the lifetime of an edition. Any updates that we know of for this guide will be on the Cicerone website (www.cicerone.co.uk/1235/updates), so please check before planning your trip. We also advise that you check information about transport, accommodation and shops locally. Even rights of way can be altered over time. We are always grateful for information about any discrepancies between a guidebook and the facts on the ground, sent by email to updates@cicerone.co.uk.

Register your book: To sign up to receive free updates, special offers and GPX files where available, create a Cicerone account and register your purchase via the 'My Account' tab at www.cicerone.co.uk.